HEART to Win

How Changing Your HEART Can Lead to a Seven-Figure Income

Kerry Jayne Jackson

United States, 2020

CUSTOMER TESTIMONIALS

Pamela Doe

"After losing money on the inspection process of a house purchase that fell through because of an inexperienced agent, a friend referred me to the MarketPros' website. I was lucky to find an experienced agent who truly cared more about me than her commission. She helped us find whatever we needed even after the sale ended. I was grateful to realize MarketPros' vets every agent. Thank you for creating MarketPros.com. You gave us peace of mind! MarketPros' is a sign of the times for the future of Real Estate agents."

The McManaways

"After catching one agent in a couple of lies, we found an experienced agent on MarketPros'. We were trying to buy a condo at a price we wanted to pay. The MarketPros' agent was a key factor in getting what we wanted quickly and is still looking after us even years after the sale. She was a true Marketpros."

Bev and Roy Breeling

"We originally wanted to be at the east end of Panama City Beach but after getting to know our MarketPros' agent better, she convinced us to look at the west end. We are so glad she knew the area and had the experience and confidence to help us think out of the box. She read us perfectly and discovered the lifestyle we really wanted by pointing us to an area we never really knew about. We are absolutely glad to call it home now!"

The Cargle Family
"We heard about the concept of MarketPro's after we lost money with an unscrupulous agent. We were devastated. We found a recommended agent with 20 years of experience to help us. What a difference someone with experience and expertise makes! More importantly, she was someone we could trust, who cared about us and made everything right, no matter what it took. She was a true MarketPros' agent."

Tricia and Ken—Military Relocation
"Having an agent with solid relationships within a community made all the difference in our home purchase. On a walk through the night before our house closing, we discovered a major water leak that flooded the upstairs of our potential new home. Within 12 hours, our MarketPros' agent pulled together the necessary repair team, complete with quotes, negotiated a deal on our behalf with the seller's agent, and informed the Lender as to how we could still close on time. We did. Only a MarketPros' agent could have pulled this off."

DEDICATION

This work is dedicated to my sons, Brady and Taylor.

When you were born, I had 3 wishes for you. I wanted you to be healthy, to be independent and happy in whatever you decided to do, and to experience joy by living life on your terms as you worked hard, took chances, and enjoyed the journey. I wanted you to understand what it meant to both give and receive.

You were showered with love and material things. When I failed, we lost the material things, but you still owned my unconditional love. Thank you for enduring the long car rides where we listened to motivational speakers each time I traded the Barney cassettes for Les Brown. I hope you laugh when you remember a little of both.

Writing this book is my attempt to give you a road map for the career path you choose. I hope it gives you a direction to achieve a meaningful life. I want you to know I did my best with what I knew and what I had.

Now, the ball of life is in your court. Choose what makes your heart sing. Don't be afraid to change courses if that is what it takes. Remember, dreams don't work unless you do. You have one life and you never know when it will end, so make the best of it. Never give up, because great things take time. You are totally different individuals, but you both have what it takes to succeed. I have faith that will happen.

Finally, to everyone I've ever met or done business with, thank you for our experience together. The stories and lessons I've learned, I have passed on in an effort to help others.

FOREWORD

THE WORLD OF real estate is fast-paced and volatile. The Real Estate profession is riddled with untrained, unethical, and greedy real estate agents. Add to that, the fact that thousands of people enter the profession armed with little more than a short real estate course and a simple test, and you have the ingredients for buying and selling disasters.

I wrote this book to highlight the pitfalls that expose those unsuccessful agents. I then offer hopeful remedies to struggling agents that can ensure a profitable career, even if the profession changes in the future.

To date, data shows the importance of utilizing real estate professionals, but why is it that home and commercial buyers are seeking ways to cut commission-based real estate agents? Might it be because the real estate profession has failed to respond to the needs of their customers in an effort to line their own pockets? Or is it because buyers and sellers have had bad experiences with unqualified and uncaring agents?

If well trained and tested, agents and agencies are critical to the buying and selling process. They are guides through the maze of rules and regulations, laws and associations, and financing and closing processes. Without them, buyers and sellers have little protection from predators who seek to part the client from their money.

So, how can we assure that the agent we choose to assist us with the largest purchase of our lives will care more about the client's wishes than their commission? How can we change the attitude of future buyers and sellers who show their frustration with our profession by turning to the Internet for all of their needs? How can we retain new sales representatives who might end up being great agents, but left to themselves will learn the business from a pack of greedy wolves? Where do we start the process that will ensure their success?

We look for MarketPros'.

What is MarketPros'?

MarketPros' are experienced agents with a proven track record of high standards and sales. MarketPros' is not just a term to describe a full-time, successful real estate agent. It is a change of mindset for the profession. MarketPros' are committed to restoring the reputation of real estate professionals worldwide by providing a secure platform where consumers can have confidence that the listed realtors and agents have been well vetted and are legitimate professionals, not great marketers promoting themselves as such on the Internet.

How are MarketPros' vetted?

MarketPros's agents must meet the following requirements:

- They must be full-time, licensed real estate professionals for the past five years.
- They must have lived or worked in their chosen sales area for three to five consecutive years.

- They are required to have closed at least 12 successful transactions each year for the past three years, with nothing less than an 80% positive review rating.
- They must hold to the belief that helping consumers is their main objective, knowing financial gain will come only after a trusting relationship with the client has been developed.
- Finally, a MarketPros' agent will commit to continuous growth, both in their personal and professional life. This commitment will ensure the best possible buying and selling experience for the client and the agent.

MarketPros' is not an association, though being part of MarketPros' will certainly ensure vetted agents will be leading the future of real estate. MarketPros' is an attitude that permeates an agent's very being. It's a mindset that makes a MarketPros' agent stand out from the crowd. MarketPros' is not a get-rich-quick scheme. It's not something you can buy. Instead, it's a change of attitude that takes an average agent from good to great!

In other words, becoming a MarketPros' is a modification of the "old" real estate sales way of thinking. Instead of encouraging agents to simply study a short course to learn the rules of selling real estate so they can "make money," MarketPros' offers the public a vetted system of highly motivated agents, who are guided by HEART to Win principles, that ensure a positive buying and selling experience! No more amateur salespeople bent on their commissions. MarketPros' are the agents whose purpose is to serve the client, not themselves.

Throughout this book, I hope you feel the fire that burns inside of me for this business. I have a mission. I never want another agent to enter this profession, and then find himself or herself so discouraged they quit. I don't want agents to feel they aren't being treated fairly by their agencies or realize they are not making enough money, especially since I know that the HEART to Win philosophy can change that.

The tips inside this book reveal why it is vital for an agent to become MarketPros'.

The text explains how utilizing the MarketPros' HEART to Win philosophy will be critical to professionally servicing your clients, and imperative for an agent's long-term success.

Ride with me as you learn how MarketPros' navigate the road to sales far beyond your expectations!

CHAPTER 1

Begin at the Beginning

I GREW UP in a modest working-class family. Money always seemed to be an issue in our home. I learned at an early age that if I wanted something above and beyond my necessities, it was up to me to earn the money to pay for it.

I wanted better things in life. I didn't want to settle for mediocrity. Too many people around me seemed satisfied with little. I wanted to be different, and I wanted to make a difference. So, at nine-years-old and in the middle of a harsh Canadian winter, I armed myself with my new toboggan and began transporting newspapers from door to door. I delivered my newspapers on time and with a smile, no matter the weather. Customers praised my attitude, my tenaciousness, and my timeliness. Their encouragement gave me the confidence I needed to continue my mission. I felt I was on the right track to making money.

A few weeks into my new venture, I began noticing my positive attitude was triggering my customer base to grow. One neighbor would tell another neighbor about my work ethic, and that neighbor would recommend me to yet another customer. It did not take long for me to develop an example I continued to follow throughout my remaining delivery career.

The lessons I learned about having a positive attitude, going above and beyond, and keeping promises are truths that have served me well, both as an entrepreneur and as a Real Estate Broker. I discovered the more work I took on, the harder I worked, and the better worker I became. I learned that the nicer I treated others along the way, the more money I made. It was as simple as that. Of course, I had no idea that those common traits were so uncommon in today's world.

As a child, I often wondered why many of the other kids with paper routes were not being as successful as I was. To me, hard work, done the right way made sense. I believed that doing the right thing was always the right thing to do. That truth eventually led me to buy and sell paper routes for extra money. My little paper route kept growing as I built my business on those principles. I won prize after prize for selling subscriptions. I won season tickets to the Toronto Maple Leafs games in Maple Leaf Gardens. The attention I garnished gave me the notoriety I needed to grow more business. The experience then gave me the confidence that anything I wanted to accomplish was possible.

By age ten, I sold my first paper route and purchased a bigger one. Year after year, I repeated that process. When I turned 13, I sold my profitable route in an apartment building to someone who was just starting their journey. That first venture had shown me I could be profitable following the simple principles I had honed. Even today, I think back to the initial philosophies I learned on that paper route.

Take on work others won't. Work harder at being the best. Have a good attitude. Be nice.

These same principles changed me from the little girl who once slung the Toronto Star onto neighborhood front porches into the real estate superstar I am today.

Whether you're stuck in part-time purgatory or you are a full-time seller that can't seem to crack a six or seven-figure status, this book is for you. I don't know where you are in your career. But before you advance in any endeavor, you have a choice to make. Think about the following anonymous quote, and then ask yourself, which do I have to do to be successful? Your answer might make or break you.

"The toughest choice you may ever face is to choose to walk away or try harder."

A MarketPros' Mindset
Don't be good; be great at what you do.

The same entrepreneurial spirit that guided me from a paper hustler to a multi-million dollar real estate agent can be employed to improve an agent's sales goals.

I committed to a career in real estate sales at the late age of forty. People looked at me like I was crazy. They asked, "Why in the world did you get into real estate?" I had been dabbling in real estate investments for a while when my broker commented that I'd make a great real estate agent. He said, "You're already doing all the work for yourself. I'm just sitting back, making all the commission." His comments were what I needed to hear. That moment made me reflect on my childhood paper route success and caused me to recall the lessons I'd learned. So, I began to take on more responsibilities. I worked harder than any other agent, yet I remembered to treat everyone I met; everywhere I went, with a kindness, they never forgot.

I would love to tell you I was immediately a force others envied. However, in my first year as a real estate agent, I found myself floating from one brokerage to another. I lasted three weeks with the first company, one month with the second and two months with the third agency. I hit a wall and was ready to quit. In that first year, with all the extra work I'd taken on and all the excitement I 'd brought to my job, I barely made $30,000. Having earned a six-figure income in a career where I was an underling, I felt like a failure. A loser.

The confidence I entered into the real estate field with quickly evaporated. There were nights I would lie awake in bed crying. I'd ask myself, "What have I done? I gave up on a six-figure opportunity, for what? To make thirty grand?" Being the primary breadwinner with two small children and a husband who had just launched a business of his own, I felt as though I'd let my family down. I didn't know what to do. I was discouraged and disgusted.

For the fourth time during my first 12 months selling real estate, I switched agencies. Again. This time Coldwell Banker Realty hired me. I knew I had to do something different from what I'd done at past agencies.

Because there wasn't enough room for each agent to have their own space, I was placed in a cubicle with another agent. The tight quarters turned out to be a blessing in disguise. I decided to sit quietly and observe my fellow agent rather than jumping at every phone call or walk-in. His phone rang continually. I took notes and listened carefully. I noticed that he kept his promises to his clients and really tended to every step of the sales process. He laughed a lot and never seemed in a hurry when he was with customers. The clients that came to the office were greeted like old friends and then I realized many of them were. He'd cultivated those relationships with hard work and kindness.

That was a watershed moment. In that tiny office, I reclaimed the confidence I'd lost in the real estate business and in myself. Watching my partner, I understood that his success had left me hints, clues I recognized from my previous careers in sales. I began modeling my new mentors' habits and polished the skills I'd used in my childhood and throughout my entire working life.

As new clients appeared, I made an important decision to become both help to my clients, and a resource for others around me. By doing so, I knew I'd become a valuable asset to the company and could show myself to be a worker who cared about lifting the team rather than selfishly considering my own pocketbook.

At the beginning of this process, I didn't make much money. I was busy doing the groundwork necessary for a successful career. I was learning everything I could about my area and creating a network of relationships that continue to serve me to this day. Sales did not climb rapidly, but they grew every month. I stayed busy building a strong foundation for future growth. Learning. A year later, I received my Broker's license and looked forward to opening my own brokerage firm.

Soon I surpassed the sales goals of my office buddy. He wasn't jealous. He was pleased I'd learned to be different, as he was, from most real estate agents. Today, I'm a million-dollar real estate agent. I can generate over a hundred thousand dollars a month in income. I'm often one of the Top 10 earners in my association and am one of the Top 2 women agents.

It hasn't been a cakewalk. The real estate business is tough. After 20 years in this industry, I have seen agents steal other agent's sales. I have seen cheating and lying concerning commissions. Real estate is a cutthroat business. Be prepared and realize that becoming a MarketPros' agent will alleviate the possibility of having to work with unscrupulous sales people!

A MarketPros' Mindset
It's not about you

Some people care more about the possibility of making a large commission than they do about fulfilling their client's needs. Some agents will lie to clients to close a sale. Some agents will encourage a buyer to put in an offer on a property the agent knows is not right for the client. And the truth is, some agents are lazy. They show a house, write the contract, get the commission, and that's it. Never to be heard from again.

But you know what? Even knowing these things doesn't mean we have to compete with these agents. I love competition. I love being competitive. Yet, in this industry, you can't be competitive and win. Sure, that may sound like a paradox, but hear me out. You can't compete against other agents. That isn't a winning philosophy. Instead, compete with the best version of yourself.

How do we do that? Measure *your* capabilities and *your* potential, not someone else's. Comparing yourself to another agent is misdirected energy.

In high school, I was a sprinter on a relay team. The event is comprised of a two-person or four-person team. Our job was to run a portion of the race as fast as we could before passing off a baton to the next runner.

One of the lessons our coach taught us was never to look back. To do so was to cause you to slow down. She explained we would never win if we were always looking back at the competition. Instead, she coached us to position our hand to receive the baton and keep moving forward.

That principle applies to the real estate profession. Never turn around and look at what other agents are selling. If anything, look forward to meeting them, look forward to sharing your knowledge, look forward to partnering with agents that are willing to work with you instead of working against you.

Real estate sales can have a dark side, but only for those who are competing. A good agent is not here to compete. They are here to complete. In other words, they are here to complete personal goals, complete partnerships with other agents, and completely service and satisfy the client.

What does completion look like? How do we know when we are completing our goals instead of competing with other agents? Remember when I revealed earlier how the praises of my customers were a source of encouragement to me? That kind of inspirational feedback is evidence you're doing the right thing in the right way. That praise might come as a review, an email, small tokens of appreciation, or other agents sending 'Thank You' cards for working with them.

An example of the power of appreciation came after I opened my real estate agency. For four years, I had no sign on the front of my business. I invested very little in marketing. I wasn't aware of social media. I didn't even have a list of my existing clients. In fact, looking back now, I made plenty of mistakes. Yet, even with those mistakes, the foundation I'd created working with my previous agency propelled my sales upward.

Friends and family often asked me how I was making so much money? Where were my clients coming from? I hadn't thought about it. I wasn't focused on being successful. I stayed focused on the process of giving my best and doing the right thing.

Yet, their questions made me reflect on my path to my financial freedom. I began to think about the process I'd created that took me from a broke, scared agent to creating a revenue stream of income that was regularly six-figures a month. I took a few days off and found a quiet little place to consider the successful road I'd created. I jotted notes, listed out my successes and failures, and made a list of future goals.

The HEART to Win philosophy erupted out of that reflection and drove my passion to share the lessons I have learned.

A MarketPros' Mindset
Focus on the client's needs not your commission

Why did I use the acronym HEART? Mark Twain famously said, *"It's not the size of the dog in the fight; it's the size of the fight in the dog."* I knew it took heart to fight, and I was a fighter! To be a successful real estate agent, you have to put your whole being into the business. You have to have a fire in your soul and be willing to fight to improve yourself.

Though I am older now, I still have the same passion for sharing this message as I did when I was young. Once agents employ the principles I am suggesting, there will be no reason to quit this profession, feel you aren't being treated fairly, or have an excuse for not making good money. If you get into the real estate profession and you follow the HEART to Win principles, I know it will change your life.

For instance, if you're making $50,000 a year, the HEART to Win philosophy can move you to $100,000 a year. If you've plateaued making $100,000 a year, you'll soon be able to break that barrier and achieve $400,000 a year. And if you believe a million dollars a year is possible, you'll accomplish that too.

A MarketPros' Mindset
What one man can do, another can too.

You can do this. I'm a firm believer that anything one person can do, another can do. If the HEART method skyrocketed my success, then it can surely be the catalyst for yours as well. Just ask yourself one question. Do you have the HEART to Win?

I have experienced the fact that applying the HEART principles changed my income from $50,000 a year to $100,000 a year. When I got at $100,000 a year, I continued to apply the HEART philosophy and broke the barrier to make $400,000 a year. And when I began to believe I could earn a million dollars a year, it became possible. This book is not a get-rich-quick scheme. HEART to Win is a process that will guide those who are committed to a career in real estate to achieve goals they never thought possible.

CHAPTER 2

Habits of Success

ONCE UPON A time not so long ago, I achieved the kind of success the HEART to Win principles afford those who practice them. For a while, I had a picture-perfect life. I lived in a gorgeous house, drove a fancy car, partied on our boat with clients and friends. I had it all. Then, 2008 arrived. The fast-paced real estate market had created an artificial housing bubble exacerbated by the stock market crash.

This crisis affected the entire real estate industry in historically devastating ways. Even today, we still feel the negative effects on consumer behavior. In my region alone, 70% of agents barely made a suitable living. Many went broke, and eventually left the profession choosing steady paying jobs over commission-based income.

As if that wasn't enough, 2010 brought the infamous BP oil spill to the entire Gulf Coast region of Florida. Suddenly, right when I thought I was almost out of the carnage of the 2008 real estate crash and could put the crisis behind me, the oil spill created a further downturn in our local economy.

Agents began leaving our area in droves; most believing the real estate business would never recover.

Personally, I was fighting to save my credit score and my reputation. I was writing checks in excess of forty-five thousand dollars a month for mortgages on 17 homes I'd sold, just to help people hold on to them. With little hope in sight, owners who had no way to pay me back eventually abandoned those 17 homes. My CPA told me I had to stop paying the mortgages. My bank account had dwindled to next to nothing. I had to surrender the properties after a three-year battle to try and salvage what I'd built. I ended up filing for bankruptcy at 55-years-old. I lost two to three million dollars of my own money.

But just as these crises tore the community apart, it also tore my financial world apart.

I lost my home.
I lost my income.
I lost my savings.
I lost all of the material things that, at one time, meant a lot to me.

But I didn't lose HEART.

My husband had a hard time handling the stress. He started drinking. He drove himself into the dark cloud of addiction, and for three years, he remained there. I had nowhere to turn. At that lowest point, I took control of my own life and filed for a divorce. I had two sons to care for and nowhere to turn.

Realizing I had no one to depend on but me, I focused on the philosophy that had lifted me out of poverty once before. I knew there was something better ahead for me. My mindset was being tested. Looking back, I realized this dark lesson was less about money, and more about the strength within that keeps me going forward. I began to look at my life. I had my health and my sons, and I still had the skills and knowledge that had taken me on a beautiful ride. I knew the vulnerability I was feeling would be short-lived.

A MarketPro's Mindset
With a HEART to Win, you can turn your setback reasons into comeback seasons.

I kept an attitude that if I could reach my goals once, I could do it again. And I did, but the next time I did things very different. It was a lesson I discovered that made the difference between selling real estate and developing habits that would drive me to become a seven-figure real estate agent.

"What you call a crisis, God calls a classroom."
Dr. Keith Johnson

It was during my personal downturn that the HEART method originated. The HEART philosophy helped me recover from the crisis and move forward. I began to understand the strength and power of personal growth. The old adage that said, *"When the student is ready, the teacher appears,"* was timely for me.

I was more than ready to look to the future and reached out for my new mindset like that high school sprinter receiving a baton. The HEART to Win philosophy held me steady through the struggles in my personal and business life. I started looking at each crisis as a lesson that became instrumental in my personal growth.

I became a sponge. I absorbed every ounce of wisdom using social media, and online podcasts, as well as books on business subjects. I attended seminars that helped me determine upcoming sales trends. I asked questions of mentors, sales masters, and financial coaches, all people who took their time to encourage me to grow personally, professionally, and financially. In the end, I found value in the pain I had to go through.

I was determined never to look back.

CHAPTER 3

A HEART to Win Philosophy

SO, WHAT IS the HEART to Win philosophy, and how can you attain the skills you need to grow your wealth using this method?

The word HEART is an acronym for Habit, Ethics, Attitude, Resilience, and Trust.

Let me break this down and explain the way each of these words can make a difference in your life.

The H in HEART is Habit.

You have to make personal growth a habit. It is not a line on a checklist. It is not a priority. A habit is a fixed practice that is non-negotiable. It's digging a well before you're thirsty so that you will never go thirsty again. It's putting down footings that will hold up a skyscraper. Why? Because hard work is a habit, and the foundation must be strong. It wasn't by accident that I lost everything and yet, was able to rebuild the empire I once had to something beyond anything I believed could be done. Success was my second nature.

A MarketPro's Mindset
Winning habits make your success inevitable.

Maybe you've heard that it takes 21 days to form a habit. This wives tale stemmed from an observation made during the 1950's. Surgeon Maxwell Maltz discovered after a surgical procedure; it took a minimum of 21 days for a patient to get used to their new reality. For some, that adage might be true, but I have found it takes a bit longer to lock a lifelong habit in.

Phillippa Lally, a health psychology researcher at the University College in London, England, had a different, more realistic view. She used recent research and published her findings in the European Journal of Social Psychology. After observing 96 participants over 12 weeks, Lally discovered the average person was able to form their newly chosen habit in 66 days.

Whatever time it takes for you to form a habit, be sure to dedicate yourself to doing so if you want to reach that seven-figure income in real estate.

Here are three particular habits that have served me well. Once you begin practicing these habits, stay with them for at least two months. The results will be amazing!

Habit #1 - Personal Growth

What does a personal growth habit look like?

- It's finding a mentor who can motivate you or a coach that will help you clarify your vision and hold you accountable to complete your goals
- It's reading ten pages-a-day of a non-fiction book about

successful business leaders who share motivational stories
- It's devouring every relevant learning experience, be it a podcast, a seminar, or a conference. Let learning become an obsession. The cost or distance becomes part of the educational process that will pay off down the road.
- It's learning from others. Take the most successful agent out to lunch and ask questions and then listen.

Habit #2 - Preparation

Preparation is crucial. Clients expect MarketPros' to be prepared for all of the questions they might have. You can have a great attitude, wear designer suits and read all the right books, but if you're not prepared with the knowledge and experience you need to serve your client, you'll never reach a seven-figure income.

To be truly prepared you have to ask yourself some basic questions:

- What elementary information have you gathered for your clients *before* you get to your appointment? Do you have facts and figures, community information, neighborhood comparisons, or crime reports on hand?
- Have you asked your client all the right questions?
- Do you know how to get to the property?
- Have you inquired about the property surroundings or what areas might be slated for development nearby?
- Have you talked to other agents to gain additional bits of information that might be useful to your client?
- Do you know the taxes on the given home you are showing or the condo fees for properties in an association?
- Do you have a pulse on the city or neighborhood that you can share?

- Did you pull comps and analyze them?
- Did you ask yourself what you could do to make this showing an event?
- How far away will the client be from their workplace, hospitals, airports, and fire stations?
- What schools or shopping areas are close to the home?

The answers you are prepared to give will show you are a true professional!

When I wake up in the morning, I prepare myself. I exercise to get in the right frame of mind. I dress well. I eat a healthy breakfast and train my mind for the coming day. I find that something special happens to my confidence when I try to be my best. My confidence and appearance position me as an expert. A force to be reckoned with. An authority.

I ask myself how many people can I help today or what can I do to help this person the most? That is where my preparation starts.

I'm doing business for recent development in my area where I sell a lot of condos. There is a new park being built near the condo development. I stay up to date on the construction of that park. I know when the building will be completed, what the economic impact is going to be, and how it's going to benefit or harm the client that is looking for a place in that area.

My preparation includes understanding zoning laws. If I'm talking to investors, I need to know if they will be able to have daily or weekly vacation rentals in specific neighborhoods. If the property is a condo, are owners or renters allowed to have pets? Being prepared to answer questions like this are critical to showing professionalism.

I recently read a trade article of a woman who lost her real estate license for six months because she told somebody they could have a dog in a condominium townhouse community, where no dogs were allowed. The people closed on the house. On moving day, the new owners showed up in the truck with their dog. The misinformation resulted in unhappy clients and an agent whose license was suspended as a result. MarketPros' are always prepared for their clients!

A MarketPros' Mindset
The difference between a professional and an amateur is preparation.

Another example came from a condominium community where I once lived. Every few days, I would notice potential clients walking around with an agent. Most times, the agent met the client at the property only to find the agent had not notified the client that they needed a gate code to get in. Once the agent arrived, the agent directed the client from building to building as they searched for the right unit. Had the agent driven to the property the day before, they would have looked more professional rather than looking like the rookie the client had to deal with.

It is a common-sense action for an agent to visit a property well ahead of the client in order to show expertise. There's nothing worse than the blind leading the blind. You waste their time and yours, and that mistake may cost you money and your reputation.

Habit #3 - Priority

Priority is focusing on serving the client you're with and doing what's best for them, not you. In the moment you are working with a customer, whether speaking on the phone, sending an email or in a meeting face-to-face, give the client first place. Don't interrupt them to take a phone call, answer someone else's question, or read a text. Connect with their eyes. Show the client that they are important to you in that moment.

For instance, I never send a generic email. My emails are personal because I have taken the time to listen to what the client wants. I repeat what they say to be sure they understand I have heard their concerns and desires. I take notes. I learn a lot about them. I know whether they like dogs or horses, what their sense of humor is like, what interests they have, and their pet peeves. I build a rapport so the next time we have contact, I can convey some of what I have learned about them into a message that shows I care. Knowing more about who they are, allows me to show a higher level of personalization and that personalization turns into profit.

An example of how agents fail in this respect is when a client says, "My budget is $250,000." A short time later, the agent shows the client homes that are selling for $400,000. A move like that shows the agent did not hear the client or assumes the client is willing to spend more. On the opposite spectrum, an agent might show client homes in the customer's requested price range when the client realizes they really could pay more than they first budgeted. They drop the agent clues when they say, "Oh, my taste is a bit more expensive than this." If an agent is not listening closely, they can miss these clues and telegraph to the client that they are not being heard.

Listening carefully and asking the right questions will satisfy a client that may not precisely know what they want. As an agent, you have to ask detailed questions about your client's budget and be truthful about neighborhoods, schools, and square footage. In other words, make your client's needs your priority, not your commission.

Lose the 'what's in it for me' mindset. Stop being a narcissist. Start focusing on your client. Remember Alec Baldwin's famous line in the film Glengarry Glenross, *"ABC, Always Be Closing?"* He had it wrong. The saying should read, "Always be serving." Serving is the only way to make sure your sales pipeline is full enough to be constantly closing sales. Find a way to make your client's day. That is what it means to go above and beyond. Sales aren't about being a salesman; it is about being a decent human.

A MarketPros' Mindset
The person I am presenting on the outside, Is the person I am enjoying living with on the Inside!

The former CEO of Chrysler Corporation, once said, *"I only wish I could find an institute that teaches people how to listen."* Business people need to listen at least as much as they talk. Too many people fail to realize that real communication goes in both directions. A person who feels listened to is more likely to understand their ideas are being heard. Listening is a sign of respect. It makes a person feel valued. Without listening, how do you even know what to sell them?

A MarketPros' Mindset
Big egos have little ears.

Here is another tip. Become your client's real estate coach. Ask them what needs they have and then deliver what they want. Listening carefully and taking notes during your first conversation will ensure you have the right knowledge to satisfy your client's needs. That way you can encourage the client in the direction that will be best suited to their wishes.

How do you begin that first conversation? Start by asking your clients about themselves. People enjoy talking about themselves. They like sharing a little about their lives, their children, and their dreams. Those conversations then give an agent hints they can file away to show the client they care. It is during that very first discussion where customers learn to trust you. Down the road, use these rapport-building moments to show the client you were listening and are able to respond to their needs.

Having a HEART to Win means discovering the heart of your client. Discovering what triggers their heart is done by asking questions and paying attention to what your client feels is important. True MarketPros' embrace the role of a coach in the lives of their clients. Not so of a typical salesperson.

Your clients don't want a salesperson. They want a helper. Otherwise, why would people even call real estate agents? They call us because they simply don't know how to buy a house or sell their house. We do. That's the reason they are calling us. They need our expertise. For now. The future of real estate sales is a bit uncertain, but MarketPros' are unafraid because they are prepared for change.

That is why developing good habits are so important. Forming successful habits is as much about what you should stop doing, as it is about what you should start doing. Often the things we should stop doing are hidden beneath the surface. For instance, maybe you are stuck in a pattern of negative thinking or harmful self-talk.

Frequently, it is the people who surround us, or the environment we live and work in that reinforce our shortcomings or weaknesses. Having a negative self-image can be as simple as not taking time to focus on what truly matters. Cut out the images from your past that made you think you are not worthy of being successful. Turn your back on the abuse you may have gone through. Forget the tough things people continue to remind you of. Don't let others determine the person you will become!

Whatever the case, be as ruthless about cutting out the bad memories and thought processes that haunt you as you are with kick starting the good habits you are ready to develop. Replace a bad habit with better practices, one at a time. Soon, you will see progress with the good habits you have chosen to create, and you will recognize that the bad thoughts are disappearing.

CHAPTER 4

Charisma or Character?

IN EVERY SALES profession, there is always a question that is tossed around in one form or another. Which trait is more critical: Charisma or Character? Should you be a magnetic personality that attracts clients, or should you develop your integrity to better serve clients?

Successful agents have both. They are not mutually exclusive. In an effort to protect our charisma, sometimes, our character gets in the way, and we end up tripping over it. It's happened to me, and it will happen to you. When you make a mistake, be sure you acknowledge that before moving on. Everyone shows his or her human side at one time or another. It's okay. Yet, you need to recognize your misstep and look for ways to correct it to retain the trust your client has bestowed on you.

A MarketPros' Mindset
Charisma and character are not mutually exclusive qualities.

These business mistakes usually come in the form of shortcuts. When I first began my career in this profession, I took shortcuts that eventually cost my clients or me money. For instance, a client once asked me a simple question of which I should have known the answer. She asked, "Is grounds keeping included in the HOA fee?" Without knowing the correct answer, I gave them the response they wanted to hear. I said, "Yes," and we went to closing. I should have explained that I didn't know for sure, but I would get them an immediate answer. Shortly after the house closing, a ticket was issued to my clients because their grass was too long. The clients called to inform me that when they went to complain about the ticket, they learned *they* were responsible for their lawn maintenance. I was embarrassed but worse; I could have had my license suspended. I was fortunate. I got away with paying their fine, a bruised ego and a lesson learned. I was lucky that my shortcut didn't end up in a lawsuit.

A good litmus test you can use to determine if you're taking a shortcut is to ask yourself, "Am I making this decision based on my commission, or the well-being of my client?" Being honest with yourself will let you know where your heart is.

A MarketPro's Mindset
Never make a commission-based decision

A common issue when selling condominiums is underestimating upcoming assessments. Assessments are a bad word in real estate. Agents often deflect answers or take shortcuts when discussing assessments with new clients. The worst thing an agent can do is take a shortcut if a client asks, "Are there any pending assessments coming up?" An agent's reply should be honest and based upon the due diligence performed *before* they meet with a client. Anything less than honesty might end up in a lawsuit.

If you don't know an answer, seek them out. Ask questions of the association, such as, "Are there assessments or pending litigation I need to be aware if I am working with a new buyer?" Follow up with the client in writing to assure the buyer fully understands you have communicated the correct answer. This way the buyer can make an informed decision, now armed with the proper information.

An example of how to handle the buyer's question would be to send an email to the potential buyer saying, "Based on our conversation today, I called Jackie Smith, the association manager, to inquire about any pending assessments or litigation. She assured me that for the foreseeable future, no assessments or litigation are pending. I hope this information will satisfactorily answer your question. Thank you for putting your trust in me." Make sure you receive a response that you can file to assure no misinterpretations of their request. Which brings us to the next letter in the HEART acronym.

CHAPTER 5

Ethics

The E in the HEART Method refers to your Ethics.

ETHICS IS ONE of the most essential qualities of a seven-figure real estate professional. As we have seen, shortcuts and lying to customers in an effort to make more money is what damages the reputation of most realtors.

I make sure I am operating with complete honesty, telling clients the pros and cons of a property as I am showing it. Your preparation will keep you well informed of possible pitfalls of the property, as well as the upgrades any seller wants you to notice. Make sure you acknowledge the cons of a property first. It builds your credibility and shows you have done your homework. Showing your client that you are well prepared and unafraid to share everything you know about a property will build trust for both buyers and sellers.

For example, you might explain to a client who is buying a condominium, "You are going to see construction on some of the balconies. That is because there was a construction defect lawsuit filed by the association seven years ago, which the association won. The association is now using the funds they received from the suit to complete the necessary repairs. " Clients may ask for more information on the lawsuit. Be prepared with as much information as you can find. Your knowledge shows that you are well prepared to address their concerns and give them further confidence in your professional skills and their home purchase.

Another side of ethics you should consider is your reputation within the industry. That reputation begins in the office in which you work. In other words, it's how you interact with other agents and staff as well as how you treat them.

Here is an example of what I mean. If a client comes to you and tells you they are working with another agent in your office, don't say what a poor agent they are, whether true or not. Frequently other agents may say, "That is not a problem. You don't have to work with them. We are all a team." In the real estate business that is back-dooring another agent. It is unethical, despite any opinion you might have of that agent. MarketPros' offer assistance and then notify the other agent about the conversation. They keep everything on the up and up. I will say that if a client absolutely says "I don't trust them" or "I won't work with them" then by all means, take them on and show them how MarketPros' conduct business in the Real Estate industry.

In this profession, everyone remembers when a fellow professional shows a weak moral spirit and they repeat the agent's transgressions to other professionals.

Reputation, in this industry, is essential. It becomes even more critical when a multiple offer situation arises. If you are dealing with brokers or agents that know how unethical you have been when dealing with clients and agencies, do you think the other agents aren't going to remind the seller and buyer about your past dealings? Think about that. Local real estate dealings are public in communities. An unethical agent won't last long among real estate agents who are ethical. Keep your character clean. That is what MarketPros' strive for.

If you're unsure what character looks like, observe your actions when no one is watching. It's integrity. Remember that math term *integer*? It means whole. It's where we get the word integrity. Having integrity means working with your whole heart. Whether you're alone in the office or entertaining dozens at an open house, you bring your whole self to the situation. It means you'll be honest and strive to do the right thing whether you are alone or in a crowd.

A MarketPros' Mindset
Nothing Changes Until You Lift Your Standards

Looking at the importance of being an ethical agent means you have to think about the reason you chose this profession. It means you have to be better than the agent across the hall. It means you have to have standards that exceed expectations. My challenge to you is to raise your standard. Stop taking shortcuts. Never run the risk of ruining your reputation or the reputation of other agents, as it affects the industry as a whole.

That's one of the reasons I launched MarketPros'. It is an effort to protect and to raise the stature of agents in our industry. To do that, we need to operate with a higher sense of ethics than the industry currently requires or operates in.

Ethics is an essential characteristic of MarketPros'. Having a strong work ethic protects clients and lifts industry standards. Weak ethical principles may harm people financially and possibly place them in unsafe situations. Focusing on internal, rather than external qualities is one way agents can buoy the entire profession.

Instead of building a rock-solid value system, our profession seems to be chasing the next closing technique or future trending technology. These surface-level distractions hinder success if they are not built upon a solid foundation of moral ethics.

I used to be the President of the Board for a condo owners association. When I showed people condominiums, I always brought up the worst things about living there first. I started conversations by telling clients about my experience living in one of the condos. I let them know about pending litigation and a possible dues increase as association maintenance costs were rising. I explained that the association board could be inflexible, where rules were concerned. I also explained only one pet was allowed, as well as explaining certain dog breeds were not allowed. I told customers that the condo was not child-friendly though many owners entertained grandchildren frequently.

As we walked, I then began to point out the positive aspects of the community. It had the largest swimming pool in the county. Dues were low in comparison to surrounding condo communities. Most units had one more bathroom compared to any other units in the city, and living was all on one level, including the parking garage. The grounds were lovely and well kept, and the location was less than a mile from the beach.

When we completed our tour, I welcomed the potential buyers to walk the property on their own. I encouraged them to stop residents at the pool, mailbox, or in the fitness center and ask them how they liked living there. Those small steps ensured I slept better at night knowing my client was fully aware of the good, the bad, and ugly of homeownership in a condo community environment. I sold 40 of the 48 units available in 18 months. Why was I the top seller? People trusted me!

In the real estate profession, we have a Code of Ethics that was written in 1913, long before they created the testing and licensing we have today. I had to take an ethics course and then be tested every two years on ethics to keep my license valid. As an agent, today, are you doing what you need to do to keep the 17 articles in the Code of Ethics viable for your everyday business dealings? The Code still matters.

Although we were among the first professions to have a code of ethics, today, most industries model their code of conduct around our basic foundation. Lawyers, social workers, nurses, travel agents, even athletes from various sports have mimicked what we realized was foundational. But, who is in charge of enforcing the ethical values we swore to uphold? Who steps in when an agent is behaving in a way that is hurting their clientele? Is there any justice for the client who does not understand what is happening?

Yes, there is, but it is not always found within the governing NAR association.

In this era of technology, clients instead turn to social media. They plaster their complaints on Facebook, on Instagram, and on business websites. They write letters, make phone calls, and post negative reviews. But even more important than writing their complaints on technological outlets, they tell their friends, their relatives, and their neighbors.

Why is this client behavior so important to an agent? It is crucial because of the 80/20 marketing rule. Eighty percent of your business will always come from 20 percent of your base. It is a proven fact. In other words, if you lose one customer because you focused more on your commission than you did on your client, you lowered your ethical standards and now stand to lose a good percentage of future sales. Why? Because you'll lose a referral stream and that referral stream is necessary for your earnings growth.

I do want to stress to you that there is no such thing as 'real estate ethics.'

Wait; what? You heard me right. There is no such thing as business ethics, real estate ethics, or any other alternate version.

There are simply Ethics.

In other words, doing what is right is always right, and doing what is wrong is still wrong. Ethics encompasses your whole being. It is innate to your personality. Yet, with practice, it can be changed. Focus on doing the right thing— all the time—no matter what.

We all know of people who seem to have ethical behavior at home or in their church, yet outside of those entities, they often use entirely different standards of morality. That is where MarketPros' stands out. MarketPros' realize that no matter where they are or what situation they are in; they are always choosing to do the right thing. It's a conscious choice they live by that does not go unnoticed by those with whom they interact.

A MarketPros' Mindset
Tough moral challenges come down to personal ethics.

A title company once told me they'd dealt with several agents whose clients, at closing, remarked, "I will never do business with that agent again." I knew those agents, and by all appearances, I knew I'd heard negative things about them before. One of those agents seemed to have all of the foreclosure listings in the region, so anyone new to the area might assume he was good. He had flashy ads plastered all over town and testimonials on his website that made the unsuspecting client think he was the best agent in the area. That was not the case. Though he made money for himself and his broker in the short term, he was not successful at retaining his clients. He wasn't a MarketPros', nor did he receive referrals. His clients were what other agents felt were "one and done" clients. It didn't take long before he moved out of state; unable to escape the unethical reputation he had built. Those who choose to operate at such a low standard will never have the ability to make it long term in any business, especially in real estate. Remember, you can buy all the ads you want, but you cannot buy a good reputation.

Instead, look to those who choose to unselfishly commit to the career of real estate. Look for ways they give, rather than receive. That old Biblical adage is common sense and, in the end, offers more than it takes away. Zig Zigler once said, *"You can have everything in life you want, if you will just help others get what they want."*

As agents, we've all had clients who come to us for help even though they don't buy right away. Some never buy. Most of us have also had agents who reach out to us with questions when they learn our expertise in niche markets. In these instances, behaving ethically comes down to choosing to serve someone who may never be able to return the favor. I love the words of Denzel Washington when he said, *"At the end it's not about what you have or even what you've accomplished. It's about who you've lifted up, who you've made better. It's about what you've given back."* So share what you know and do what you can to lift others.

Here is an example of a small experiment in ethical behavior I tried years ago. I love pink. Pink is a bright color that makes others smile. I like to wear the color pink, and by doing so, other agents recognize it's "my" color. During my experiment, each time I drove by a half-cocked For Sale sign or a real estate sign that was lying flat on the ground in front of another agent's listing, I stopped and corrected the issue using a ball of pink wool twine. That pink twine alerted other agents that I had corrected an item that was important to their client without ever asking for their thanks. Yet, agents and home sellers alike noticed and rewarded me with kudos.

My experiment was just one way I learned to show others I was a team player. But the way you show others you care might arrive in one of a hundred little things you encounter on your daily travels. It might be sending a fellow agent a thank you note or it might come by dropping off a pizza to a new buyer. You might even offer to pull the listing agent's sign off the yard for your new buyer. These small gestures make a difference to so many and often result in future business.

Ethical team players ask themselves, "If this was my listing, would I be grateful to another agent who helped me look good in front of my client?" The answer would be a resounding, "yes!" That's the goal. Be an ethical agent in our profession, and it won't go unnoticed.

A MarketPros' Mindset
When it comes to ethics, MarketPros' operate from the inside out.

In a world where words such as truth, justice, and right or wrong are seemingly subjective, how can we be sure we are doing the right thing? The way I conduct myself is by adhering to what I call the following Golden Rules of Real Estate.

My 10 Golden Rules of Real Estate

1. Be Honest. The old cliché that says, "if they don't ask, don't say anything," does not apply in this profession. Always put the truth out there even if the client doesn't ask.

2. Do what you promise you are going to do. If you can't follow through, call the client and let them know. Then direct them to someone who can fulfill what you promised. Vulnerability goes a long way.

3. Appear for closings if the buyers are there. Appear for home inspections and appraisals if they are not.

4. Get along with other agents and treat them with respect; even if you don't agree with the way they conduct business.

5. If you make a mistake, admit it, own it, and when necessary, pay for it.

6. Don't fake it until you make it. Always ask questions until you have the correct answer.

7. If a customer calls and mentions they are working with another agent, but they have decided to call you with questions, be courteous with your answers, then call the

original agent to let them know about your customers concerns. Don't put the client in a bad situation. They may not understand real estate protocols. Help them reconnect with their agent unless they make it known they will no longer work with that agent. After that, it is up to you to ensure they have a better experience.

8. If you see another agent's sign has fallen down, a vacant house that has a window open, or pool low on water, call the other agent and offer to help. Don't ignore an issue just because it is not your issue.

9. Offer to pay for items that will help your clients sell their home and simply ask them to reimburse you at closing.

10. Follow the Golden Rule. Do unto others, as you would want them to do unto you.

The key to understanding the basis of any Code of Ethics is to realize you just need to do the right thing, all the time, every time.

I once read a list of seemingly successful people who died early, committed suicide, or went to prison because they consistently went for the gold instead of the Golden Rule. People from Wall Street, Enron, Worldcom, and Tyco. There are also real estate agents or title company personnel from all over the country who have crossed that ethical line and gone to prison for doing things that might have brought them the gold, but violated the Golden Rule. Don't be one of those people.

Instead, follow the simple principals in the HEART philosophy that MarketPros' follow. HEART principles are not just a way to work; they are a way of life.

CHAPTER 6

Attitude: The Difference Between Winning and Losing

WINSTON CHURCHILL, REGARDED as the most significant British citizen of all time, didn't start famous. His father wanted his son to become an attorney but thought Churchill to be mentally challenged. Winston, a stutterer who regularly ranked at the bottom of his class, failed sixth grade. It took him three years to graduate to the next level in math. Because of this setback, both Oxford and Cambridge University rejected his application for admittance.

Churchill's father encouraged him to join the Army. Following his father's advice, he applied to the Royal Military College at Sandhurst. Once again, he failed the entrance exam, not just once, but twice. After a full season of tutoring and studying, he passed the test on his third try.

After graduation, Winston joined the British Army. The career seemed to fit him well. By 1911, he became First Lord of the Admiralty, filling that position for the following four years. In 1915, during the First World War, Churchill was the mastermind behind a losing battle, historically referred to as the Gallipoli Disaster. Although some argued the fault for the disaster fell on the tactical and logistics commanders, Churchill took full responsibility for the loss, resulting in a demotion in rank. Not long after his demotion, Churchill lamented to the news media, *"I am finished. It's over for me."*

His lamentation proved to be far from the truth, as a short time later, Churchill held a variety of positions and demonstrated his value as commander. When World War II began, Churchill was appointed to First Lord of the Admiralty again, even becoming a member of the War Cabinet. Early in the war, Neville Chamberlain, the British prime minister at the time, resigned. It was Winston who was the obvious choice to replace Neville. He accepted the position and led England to victory. Despite Churchill's success, he was heavily defeated in his bid for prime minister in 1945. Many historians speculate that his success as a wartime leader may have led people to believe Churchill could not perform during a time of peace.

However, six years later, Churchill once again became prime minister. It was a role he occupied until his retirement in 1955. In 1953, the Nobel Prize in Literature was awarded to Sir Winston Leonard Spencer Churchill for "his mastery of historical and biographical description as well as for brilliant oratory in defending exalted human values." From failure and rejection to prime minister of the United Kingdom, Winston Churchill is still widely regarded as one of the most successful leaders in history.

A MarketPros' Mindset
A positive attitude will turn a pessimist into a miracle worker.

It is incredible what Winston Churchill was able to accomplish in his lifetime. His adversity makes this quote by Churchill even more extraordinary. *"Attitude is a little thing that makes a big difference."* And that brings us to the next letter in our HEART acronym.

The A in the HEART philosophy is Attitude.

An agent's attitude can be the difference between real estate being a part-time hobby or a full-time seven-figure success. When I decided to study for my real estate license, I was excited to be taking the course with a man who happened to be my age and was from the same area. We had a similar background. I found it encouraging that neither of us had any previous college education. I was giving up a successful career to delve into real estate sales, and he was a celebrated fisherman looking to make a career change.

We navigated the real estate course together. Throughout the entire training, I remembered the lessons from my childhood paper route. I kept saying to myself, "I've got to make this work. I can make this work. I will make it work. I have a great attitude. I care about people. I just need to learn the necessary rules. "

My friend's attitude was a bit different. He was a little apprehensive and scared. After class, we often talked, sharing what we had learned. While I shared the excitement of my new knowledge by saying, "Wow! I know I've chosen the right career. I know we have a lot to learn for the test, but I know I can pass it. I can see myself helping people and making a great living," my friend would respond by saying, "Boy, I don't know if I'm going to remember all this stuff. Man, I sure hope I can make a living. I don't know if I'm going to be able to make it in real estate. I might need to have a backup. Real estate license? Man, I might have to keep my fishing license." There was a distinctive attitude difference between us, a variance that took us in very different directions.

A MarketPro's Mindset
Sowing seeds of positivity always reaps definitive rewards.

Noticing my friend's poor self-talk, I realized I needed to continue planting positive seeds in my mind that assured me that choosing this career was what I wanted. I expected more of myself, and my future than my friend was willing to even dream about. I thought like a winner, while he thought like a loser. Though we had similar backgrounds, we went at our new career with different mindsets.

My friend never made it selling real estate. He never really made money at anything he did. Today, he doesn't even own a home and has found himself in an unfortunate economic situation. Yet, at one time, we were both on equal footing. How could one person fail and another become a seven-figure sales giant? I believe the difference lies in the attitudes that permeate our very being.

If you continually cultivate positive thoughts about yourself, your career, those you meet, and those you work with, you can't help but reap a great attitude. Attitude is a little thing that makes a big difference, not just in real estate, but in everything you do.

That is why MarketPros' learn to keep the principles of the HEART philosophy in balance. MarketPros' find success in cultivating the habits they need to succeed. The way they live their lives, whether at home, at work, with friends or strangers, always showcase their ethics in a way that people understand MarketPros' can be trusted.

They share their knowledge, rather than hoarding it. Assisting fellow agents who might not be as knowledgeable. They do the right thing all of the time, in every instance. MarketPros' also understand that their attitude makes a huge difference in how they see themselves, their clients, their fellow agents, and their future.

I once hired an agent who was in her 70's. Although she was a hard worker and smart as a whip when it came to real estate, she had the attitude of a warthog. It wasn't long before I realized she was losing us more clients than she was bringing in despite her vast knowledge of the industry and her strong work ethic. Her lousy attitude turned out to be more suitable for a prison matron than real estate sales. Needless to say, she didn't last long at my agency.

When you were a child, do you remember your parents saying, "You'd better get rid of that attitude," before you ever even opened your mouth? I never understood what my parents meant. I can remember wondering, "how did they know what I was thinking", as I rolled my eyes and stood slump-shouldered before them. I remember huffing back to my room as I whispered under my breath, "I didn't even say anything!"

As adults, we don't get the courtesy of being told to watch our attitude. Instead, clients show us by leaving our offices and never returning, or by choosing to work with another agent. That is why MarketPros' put themselves in a peak state of mind before they make a call or leave the office for an appointment with a client. They prepare themselves for positive experiences by doing something as simple as offering a fellow agent unsolicited help, opening a door for someone, exercising, or reading reviews from others they have served. MarketPros' have practiced the habits that will help them set a good mood for the day and have a host of attitude triggers that will keep them in that positive state of mind.

A MarketPros' Mindset
Life is not determined by what happens to you, but how you react to what happens.

Here is an example of a situation that came up during a recent sale. It challenged my MarketPros' mindset, but in the end, my HEART philosophy, once again, made a difference.

A lovely couple was moving to my area. I had worked with the couple for five days showing them multiple homes that would be an excellent fit for their needs. On the fifth day, we found a place they both loved and they immediately put it under contract. It was their dream home. Two days later, I departed for a three-day visit to California. While I was away, they decided to drive through their new neighborhood. While in the community, they spotted an open house and decided to stop by. The agent on the listing invited them in. While showing the couple around, the agent exclaimed that his listing was the best deal in the neighborhood. My clients explained they were under contract on another house in the neighborhood with another agent.

The listing agent, new to our area, told my clients that they could just cancel the deal with me and buy this new house with him—if they did so immediately. My clients loved the new house. The clients didn't recognize that the listing agent was using unethical pressure tactics to sell the house. My clients signed a second contract.

The day before I arrived home, the lender on the first deal called to inform me the listing agent had submitted another contract from my buyers. I could have copped a bad attitude in this situation. An unscrupulous agent had just back doored me. As a MarketPros' agent, I started looking for the lesson I knew was harbored in the situation.

Instead of getting annoyed with the clients, I took a few minutes to adjust my internal anger and called my buyers to ask if I had done something to upset them? They said no, not at all. They went on to explain that they had mentioned our deal several times to the other agent.

The agent's response was, "She isn't here. She didn't show you the house. Too bad. That's just how it works in this business sometimes." I appreciated the fact that they mentioned I was their agent. I also explained I would not stand in their way if this was the home they wanted.

I didn't throw in their faces the fact that once they put a house under contract; they were obligated to stick with it. I did not demand an answer as to why they went with another agent. What I did was mention that the response from the agent concerning me was not the response an ethical agent would typically give. I wished them the best of luck and asked them to contact me should they ever need anything in the future.

A MarketPros' agent would have called me and explained the situation so that we could have worked out a solution that would satisfy the client and the first home seller. This agent did not. Instead, I was left to deal with the fallout. Eventually, that agent left the business because his reputation for being ethical with clients and other agents was terrible.

Five months after this debacle, I received the following text message.

"Hi, Ms. Kerry. It's Joseph again. I always said that the next time I had a real estate need I would come to you. My brother and I got pre-approved for an investment property in Panama City Beach. Our price range is $120,000 to $150,000. Can you help us find something? I promise not to be influenced or pressured by greedy agents this time!"

Do you think if I had copped an attitude, I would have received this kind of text message? Absolutely not. Because of the MarketPros' mindset I have developed over years of cultivating a right manner, I ended up benefitting time and again from this one couple and realized how a right attitude can help you maintain relationships—or cause you to lose them.

Our attitude is the outlook with which we approach a situation. It has a significant impact on emotion. Attitudes can attract clients or repel clients. It can either impress or disappoint customers. The right attitude can hold a deal together, even if the sale seems to be headed south.

Here is another instance where attitude matters. Have you ever had a customer say, "Thanks for your time, but we are not ready to buy?" Good agents separate themselves from the pack when they hear this statement. Some quickly cut the client off sensing there is no point to continuing the contact. They fail to follow up with the client ever again. MarketPros' operate from a sense of service, not scarcity. They show understanding and make it a point to touch base with clients to show they are available should the clients' needs change.

I spent several weeks working with a lovely family looking for their next home. Instead of choosing one of the many properties I'd shown them, they bought a property that was being sold by the owner. As a MarketPros' agent, I know to expect these kinds of disappointments. I wished them well and sent them a small housewarming gift when they moved in.

My choice not to be bitter over the potential loss of a sale planted a seed of friendship that paid off within a short time. This couple ended up sending more referrals to me than any other client I have ever had. Those referrals paid out big commissions. And you know what? They still have never bought a single piece of property from me. Instead, the steady stream of referrals has turned into a steady stream of income. My good attitude made their referrals possible.

In trying to build business rapport, have you ever agreed with a client when they mentioned something negative about a property like a terrible paint color? You might be tempted to do so if the walls look like they belong in a brothel.

But a MarketPros' attitude can take clients in a different direction. MarketPros' find themselves encouraging their clients by saying, "Paint is a personal choice and quite inexpensive to change. Wouldn't you agree?" They will often share a story about another client who transformed their new home from hilariously hideous into a magnificent masterpiece.

Another instance of how attitude matters is when you have to present a lowball offer to your seller. In the beginning, the seller may say the price is too low to entertain. They might be angry that you even presented the offer to them. Many agents agree with the seller and return the contract without a further possibility of any negotiation.

MarketPros' listen as the seller voices frustration and then asks the seller to take a look at the entire contract. MarketPros' help disappointed sellers recognize acceptable requests and encourage them not to give up, but instead, to negotiate. MarketPros' assure the seller that they will speak with the buyer's agent to better understand how the buyer arrived at his offer and continually remind the seller that every contract has negotiable aspects.

MarketPros' point out the good in a contract and assists the seller in turning a seemingly unfortunate situation into something that could possibly turn into a sale. In these challenging moments, MarketPros' show off their leadership capabilities and reiterate ITT President Harold Geneen's winning mindset that says, *"Leadership is practiced not so much in words, as in attitude and actions."*

We have learned the importance of cultivating a right attitude. Now how can we help clients who struggle with their own weak outlook?

The first step is to respond to their needs in person. I know an email, a text, or a phone call are far more convenient, but these methods of contact represent only 8% of our total communication means. So, what is missing?

Our attitude indicators!

Without personal connection our clients lose out on our body language, our gestures, the tone of our voice, our presentation—all clues that give an agent a profound and surprising edge.

Over 90% of successful communication requires a face-to-face connection. According to Hubspot, an online communications blog, 72% percent of people say their impressions are impacted by how someone appears, as well as by their handshake. The Harvard Business Review implied that nonverbal cues conveyed during face-to-face contact made all the difference in how people viewed the sincerity of their interactions. The impression you leave with a client can be misconstrued in a text or email. If the client is in a foul mood, even face-to-face encounters can leave poor impressions if handled improperly.

Think about an instance where you were confronted with someone else's bad attitude? How did you react? Did you find yourself responding with a similarly sarcastic attitude? I know I have been tempted to do so. But I also know that returning a negative attitude would not only ruin my day, it would also destroy any chance I had of creating a future relationship with that person, and would ultimately result in lost sales or referrals. It might even cause me to lose a potential friendship. As a MarketPros' agent, my job is to deflect negativity and encourage people with a smile, a kind word, or a form of reassurance that shows someone cares.

MarketPros' ensure positive responses by taking the time to show clients they are mindful of their customer's needs. A smile, a firm handshake, a listening ear, and a personal appearance go a long way to shape your client's attitude. Think about it. In your own life, how many times have you unconsciously smiled back at someone when they smiled at you? We can't help ourselves. Kindness is contagious, and so are our attitudes.

A MarketPros' Mindset
When you experience a poor attitude from a client in the middle of a showing or listing appointment, it's an indication the other party disagrees with something.

Another way you can help deflect poor client attitudes is to use third party stories. Consider a client who is waffling between buying a property he loves, but who thinks the price might be a bit out of range for his financial situation. He has made an offer that the seller has just turned down. The client is upset that the seller won't accept his lower offer, an offer he can financially handle. For a short time, he is angry at the situation, not at the agent.

An inexperienced agent might try to head off a client's poor attitude by saying, "I disagree with the choice. I have been in this business for a long time. You really should listen to me. You'll be able to afford the house if you just try. Maybe you can get another job or sell something you own. You'll regret not buying this place." That kind of response is sure to turn a client off. It shows that the agent has not heard the client's concerns or fully understands the client's financial situation.

MarketPros' better handle the issue by saying, "I had a client who felt the same way you do. He agonized over his decision but decided if the seller could not meet his budget, he was better off being fiscally responsible. How about we take a look at the numbers once more and reconsider a slightly lower bid that falls in line with your financial needs. We can include a letter to the seller that explains your concerns about renovations and see if we can find some middle ground that fits both of your needs."

Let's go a step further. Imagine either of those statements blasted out in a text message or an email, versus a face-to-face meeting that allows the client to see you are sharing their concerns. An in-person encounter ensures a better outcome, a result that reflects in a customer's attitude and satisfaction.

Our experience in real estate doesn't make us wise. It is how we learn to handle both good and bad experiences that make us wise. Even the most productive agents are not without problems. Yet, MarketPros' agents who discover ways to solve issues and change attitudes grow their customer base, resulting in continual sales. They stand out from the throngs of inexperienced and self-indulging sales agents that never look beyond the money. MarketPros' understand that learning from the problems thrown into their paths gives them a self-assured attitude that exudes confidence. And that is what customers appreciate!

Agents might be astonished to learn how easy it is to solve problems when you approach the issue with the right attitude. I know. There have been moments in this business when I didn't feel like being positive. But as a MarketPros' agent, I had to tell myself that people do the best they can with what they have and what they know.

Cultivating that attitude made me realize that we are all in different places with different problems. If you can empathize, rather than criticize, you will receive a better response from clients. If you mess up, and you will, give yourself a bit of grace knowing your actions were not intentional. Instead of beating yourself up, look for the hidden lesson you are meant to learn. That is where MarketPros' understand their career is a journey.

Brian Tracy, a motivational speaker, and author reminds us to *"Develop an attitude of gratitude, and give thanks for everything that happens to you, knowing that every step forward is a step toward achieving something bigger and better than your current situation."*

A MarketPros' Mindset

Attitude is your greatest asset or your most significant liability.

Now is the time to become a MarketPros' agent with a five-star attitude. Become part of a movement where you are regarded as one of the most positive and trusted agents in your market and within the real estate profession. You can do this!

CHAPTER 7

Resilience: Fuel for the Fire

I'LL ADMIT I jumped into the real estate industry because I thought I was going to make a lot of money. During my first few months in the profession and long before the Internet and Multiple Listing Service days, I was instructed by a broker to sit in my office and wait for shoppers to come in. My boss handed me a binder that contained information about all of our listings. He told me to print the information for walk-ins when potential clients inquired about buying a home or condo.

As most agents already know, those walk-ins were few and far between. I wasn't making any money. I relied on friends and family to send me referrals. More than one time, I was ready to abandon my new career.

Driving home from the office after working endless hours, I questioned my decision to become an agent. I wanted to quit. But I didn't. I remembered the principles of my youth and resolved to take another look at some of the habits I had let slide. That is when I knew I had a HEART to Win! That brings us to the R in our HEART philosophy.

R stands for Resilience.

When someone has resilience, it means they have the capacity to recover quickly from difficulty. They evaluate the abilities, habits, and skills that made them successful in other portions of their lives, and they employ them in their present situation until they succeed once more.

If you've lived on this earth for a while, you've come to know one thing to be true. You're either headed for a crisis, in the middle of some emergency, or clawing yourself out of a mess. It's inevitable. The question then becomes, what happens when you face a roadblock? Do you use that obstacle as an excuse or an opportunity? The correct answer might be the catalyst for an excellent comeback story.

So many of us spend time and energy looking at the door that closed, rather than the window that has opened. They lament over a lost deal, a bad appraisal, or a contract withdrawal that leaves them discouraged. They cling to the bad news like a teddy bear, talking about a disaster that might have happened weeks in the past. MarketPros' look ahead. They bury the broken deals and lost revenue, and they never resurrect them again. They look for windows of opportunity and refuse to let one failed deal keep them from seeking the next good deal.

That is what resilience looks like. It is essential in the real estate business and your personal life.

My good friend Les Brown said it best when he remarked, *"When you fall, pray that you land on your back. If you can look up, you can get up."*

Unless you own the lending institution, the surveying company, the contractor, or possess a crystal ball, you're going to have to develop resilience to work in this business. Why? Because nothing is 100% predictable. Even when you have a good reputation, loads of referrals, and a good work ethic, you can't predict what will happen when other agents and vendors get involved. Therein lies the possibility of an unpredictable outcome.

I vividly remember 2008. I had been in the business for several years and had a good following. I felt on top of the world and was making a boatload of money. Suddenly, my world collapsed. A frivolous lawsuit threatened my license. A month later, the building industry took a dive, and the real estate world crumbled.

I had done nothing wrong. Everything that was happening was out of my control. By the end of the year 2009 most of the 17 properties I'd invested in as lease purchases defaulted.

When I thought things couldn't get worse, the 2010 BP oil spill occurred damaging the entire Gulf Coast and thousands of beach properties. That one event extended the recession. At the time, I was still making a six-figure income, but the income was far less than the bills I had to pay. Lenders were draining my savings.

So what did I do? I simply changed my strategy. That is what MarketPros' do. That is what all successful entrepreneurs do. When you reach a plateau in sales, in dieting, or dating, you change your outlook and search out a different strategy to make what you love to do work. You don't give up. You go back to the place you were before things broke down. You create momentum for going forward, not looking back.

In my case, I stood up for myself and hired an attorney who happened to be a client. I fought against the lies I'd been charged with. I thought to myself, "I have staying power," and I meant it. Step-by-tiny-step, I began to recover. Five years later, we won the lawsuit in the Supreme Court. I started to get my financial life on track and once again became one of the highest earning agents in the area.

A MarketPros' Mindset
Winners focus on what they want to happen, not what happens to them.

I realize that where I am today is exactly where I'm supposed to be. It is where my focus has been. Where you are now is simply a manifestation of what you have been thinking about and working toward. When you start to realize life is happening for us and not to us, what you once felt was your worst day might actually lead to your best day. MarketPros' learn how to enjoy the journey.

So, focus on the good that comes from your chosen career. You get to create new relationships. You learn new things. Your new friends like you and refer you to their friends and family. It is a very rewarding rinse, repeat cycle that creates an abundance of positive energy. It's the kind of mindset that makes you resilient. Bad things are going to happen to you. You'll be angry when they do. You'll be stressed. That much is inevitable. It's how long you choose to stay in that mental state that becomes proof of your resilience.

People who hold grudges don't have resilience. Haters don't have resilience. Resilience is an internal effort. It's not something given; it is a developed skill. When I experience catastrophes and negativity infiltrates my mind, I think about previous instances of distress and focus on the habits I have formed to ward off thoughts of depression or doubt. That is resilience.

My story and struggles are meant to be examples of the obstacles that occur in the real estate world. By sharing my story, I hope to be an inspiration to those agents who find themselves struggling in this profession.

Learning to be resilient isn't new to the real estate profession. It crosses many worlds. For instance, imagine how writers must feel as they send manuscript after manuscript to agents and publishers. For every acceptance letter they receive, most writers have collected twenty or more rejections. Yet, they keep writing.

That is resilience!

Resilience is the fire, but our thoughts are the fuel. Maybe you have experienced a downturn in the economy, perhaps a personal crisis has pulled you away from your work, or maybe your area has been hit with a natural disaster, such as a hurricane, tornado or fire.

You aren't alone. Look around. Is there another agent in your position making it work? Absolutely. They have been handed the same circumstances and yet are successfully overcoming obstacles because they have formed good habits and are prepared. They are ethical and have a great attitude. They are resilient. You can be, too! Don't give up. Being resilient means being able to change direction, change paths, and change strategies that no longer serve you. Set your HEART toward success and fuel it with the fire of resilience.

I had invested almost $2 million of my own money into those 17 lease-to-own properties and had saved a million dollars when 2008 arrived. The money dwindled quickly as the lease-to-own buyers abandoned my properties. To protect what I could, I made a quick study as to where the few homebuyers I had were coming from. It was 2010. The vacation homebuyer market had dried up. Nobody was buying. Local people were afraid to move because they were upside down in their homes. There were more foreclosures than sales. More homeowners were losing their homes then there were people buying. I realized I had to act quickly.

I changed direction, my path, and my strategy. I asked myself, "Who are the potential buyers left here?" My research revealed that many people who wanted to buy homes were living in rental properties. So instead of chasing non-existent buyers, I started focusing on renters and clients who needed affordable homes.

A MarketPro's Mindset
At the end of every recession, the government is always trying to help rebuild the economy. Find the programs that will best serve your potential clients.

I researched government-based loan options and did all I could to develop relationships with the people involved in rolling out those programs. I spent my own money to present first time home-buyer seminars and advertised the different buying programs to those who had been renting properties.

To many of my fellow agents, my plan looked like a step backward. I knew differently because I focused on my HEART philosophy. I realized that renters wanted to own their own homes. So I switched gears. And it worked! I began to sell homes, slowly at first, but soon my sales numbers increased once more. The ability to adapt is a real sign of your resilience.

Adaptation during economic vacillation is a much-needed skill in today's quickly changing world.

During our economic crisis, 60-70% of the agents in the area ultimately exited the real estate profession. This left an opportunity for the agents who were resilient enough to carry on. The 30-40% of remaining agents were the ones who made money. To this day, the MarketPros' agents who showed resiliency are now the top agents in our market.

By the time 2012 rolled around, I was still selling houses even though sales were slow. Then I had a health scare that almost took my life. Lying in a hospital ICU, I found myself repeating MarketPros' mantra. "You're not a quitter! You're a winner!"

But as I recovered, I found my personal life continued to fall apart. My spouse became an alcoholic in an effort to handle the stress of the downturn. His business failed, and he didn't have the mindset to try again. I had two boys approaching their teens, and I knew I had to make a change.

I filed for divorce before realizing the added burden of my husband not being able to earn an income had drained our bank account. That left me no choice but to declare bankruptcy. I could have given up and moved on to a new career, but I loved selling real estate, and I was no quitter. Nelson Mandela once said, "Do not judge me by my success, judge me by how many times I fell down and got back up again."

That made me recall the lessons of my track coach whose words continually drifted through my mind. *"Be competitive, but win or lose, be sure what effort was given is your best."* Those words made me understand that instead of just "going through life," I needed to keep "growing through life."

The bankruptcy was an embarrassing and painful moment for me, but it didn't keep me down. I knew I could change directions once more. I would succeed again. And I was right, because I learned to be resilient.

Being resilient means, you have learned a lesson on the way down that you can employ on the way up. Every crisis that befell me had a purpose. Through it all, one good experience arose from every ugly moment. I never knew when or how the lesson would arrive, but I always recognized the teaching moment and tucked it safely away in my heart. I called it the "Silver Lining Syndrome."

A MarketPros' Mindset
Every failure contains a lesson.

I find a "silver lining" every time I relinquish my needs for the client's dreams.

An example of a silver lining came in the form of a beautiful couple called the Rays. I'd been working with the elderly couple for a long time. Mr. Ray was entering the final chapter of his life, and his dream, as a retired Navy veteran, was to live by the water.

It took us a year to find their dream home. There were moments when he would lament, "Well, in this neighborhood, they don't allow ramps. The home I want isn't near enough to the VA hospital. The outbuildings I need are not handicap accessible." He was looking ahead. It took me only moments to realize he was going to be in a wheelchair soon and that time was of the essence When we finally found the perfect home, we all realized it was just out of their financial reach.

I knew this purchase was his dream. We had talked about the difficulty of finding a suitable house on the water that would accommodate his growing needs. When we did so his eyes would tear up. "This is where I want to spend the last chapter of my life," he said. "I want to look at the water, even if it's only a week or a month. I want to end up in a peaceful place."

I realized that in order to purchase their dream property, we would need their finances to line up perfectly, as they had little down payment. I suggested a variety of financing, eventually settling on a VA loan. I had to continually encourage Mr. Ray and his family to stay positive. "We'll never get the money," Mr. Ray would say. "My dad only wants the water property," his daughter would say. "What will we do if this deal falls through?" I explained that no matter what happened, even if the loan didn't go through, or we couldn't get the property for the price we'd hoped for, we would indeed try again until we found the perfect fit.

After finding their ideal home, we worked toward the offer. During this time I got to know the other agent. In our discussions, I discovered information about the homeowner and learned that they were motivated to sell. I shared that my client was failing and that this was their dream home. I knew we both stood to make a good commission on the sale, and I had learned there was wiggle room in the price. The other agent agreed to be flexible with commissions to complete the sale. Armed with this newfound information, we were able to negotiate the price both clients were happy with and worked together to make the Ray's dream come true. But when we completed the contract, we encountered one more challenge. The lender informed us that the home did not qualify for a VA loan.

When I hung up the phone with the lender, I quickly rifled through my mind as to how we could change this startling news into something positive. How did I make that happen? Resiliency. I'd been in this position before. The Ray's had not. But because the Ray's trusted my confidence, I assured them we'd find a way to make the sale happen.

We had many hoops to jump through. I researched a way we could show the Ray's debt-to-income ratio was good enough to secure the loan. The co-operating agent and I both lowered our commission. The lender and I worked together to correct the small things that had disqualified the home for VA approval. We made the right phone calls, filled out the necessary papers, and kept a positive attitude. The lender called a contact she'd made in the Veterans Administration years earlier, a person who ended up spearheading the effort we needed to get the Ray's property added to the list of qualifying homes. It took two months to do so, but we saw the VA loan approved and the purchase was complete. That is a benefit of working with another MarketPros' agent.

A MarketPros' Mindset
Being Resilience Helps Clients Dreams Come True

One of the critical things we did as a group was to stay positive as we worked hand-in-hand to make the deal happen. Not one of the barriers we came up against made us quit. That was pure resilience. Once I got my client on board with the confidence that we would make his dream come true, my client never gave up.

A MarketPros' Mindset
Resistance makes Resilient more persistent.

When you show you are resilient during your interactions with your clients, you're building confidence in them that will give them a reason to stay positive. When you're willing to do that, you give yourself a gift as well. What gift? The feeling of fulfillment. In the end, you'll know you added value to another person's life by helping someone's dream come true.

MarketPros' are resilient. They ask the hard questions and find solutions that make things happen when others say, "This is impossible." But the impossible is just another challenge to the resilient. "It IS possible!" That is the battle cry for the six and seven-figure MarketPros' agent.

With a MarketPros' mentality, there isn't a chance you'll quit on yourself, your profession, or your client. After all, that's not what MarketPros' do!

Instead, fuel the inner fire with resilience and add the skills you learn to your sales toolbox. Doing so shows you have a HEART to Win!

CHAPTER 8

Trust: All Eyes on the Prize

IN 1859, CHARLES Blondin walked a two-inch tightrope across Niagara Falls. The rope was anchored 180 feet above the water and was 1,100 feet long. Blondin had a habit of performing without safety nets or harnesses, believing they only invited disaster. He tiptoed on to the rope while crowds of people around him gasped. However, simply walking across the falls wasn't enough for Blondin.

On his first attempt, around 90 feet out, he stopped and sat down. With a rope tethered to his hand, he began to wrench a bottle from a boat bobbing beneath him. He stood, and as the waters below raged, tipped the bottle to his mouth and started drinking wine. He then dropped the bottle and finished his crossing only to pick up a giant camera, walk once again to the middle of the rope and take a photo of the swelling crowd. He became the first successful tightrope walker to accomplish such a remarkable stunt.

Niagara Falls would become Blondin's preferred stage, as he repeatedly performed his high wire act. With every public appearance, he became more emboldened. He made the journey backward, blindfolded, and in a potato sack. He somersaulted, bound by rope or chains, and teetered on towering stilts. But Charles still wasn't satisfied. He continually felt compelled to increase the wow-factor. The stuntman's balance was so remarkable that he often stopped mid-rope, and cooked himself an omelet.

Charles continually felt compelled to increase the wow-factor. One morning, Charles made his way across the tightrope with the usual wheelbarrow, but there was something different in it this time. He was carrying a lion.

Finally, Charles decided to perform the stunt with a human being. It was the first time Blondin had ever attempted to carry someone on his back. He was quite a performer and had a confidence that others could trust. But before that particular performance, Charles addressed the crowd. "Who believes I can walk across this rope?" he asked. The crowd roared in approval. "Who believes I can carry a wheelbarrow across this rope?" The group gave thunderous applause. "Who trusts me enough to get into the wheelbarrow and walk across with me?" The crowd's silence was deafening; until his manager, Harry Colcord, stepped forward.

Blondin admitted to his friend that the stunt could go wrong and gave Colcord one piece of advice. "We have to become one, Harry." Charles said. "We cannot try to balance on our own, no matter what happens, okay?" Pointing at the rope, he continued. "Out there, you can trust me to keep you safe." With that, Harry climbed into the wheelbarrow, and Charles pushed him across the rope. As the duo turned and began their journey back across the falls, several of the guide-lines began to break free from the high wire, but Harry never flinched. They completed their successful stunt as the crowd showered them with ear-shattering applause. After climbing out of the wheelbarrow, the two friends embraced.

That is trust in action!

Charles finished his final performance at the age of 72 after walking an estimated 10,000 miles on the tightrope oftentimes carrying others on his back.

As an agent, ask yourself this question. Who is willing to get into the wheelbarrow with you? MarketPros' cultivate a field of others willing to be a "Harry," because they've shown they can be trusted.

A MarketPros' Mindset
Trust Causes People to Follow You Even When They Face
Fear, Uncertainty, and Doubt

One of my favorite authors is Stephen Covey. He is widely known as one of the world's leading authorities on trust. He ascertains that trust is the most overlooked, misunderstood, underutilized asset that can enable performance. He explains that breaking someone's trust has a dramatic and pervasive effect. It can be far-reaching and affect more than the two people first involved. In the end, losing the confidence of someone is something one can ever replace.

Thankfully, trust is also the catalyst that can dramatically improve both personal and professional success. It is a trait that must be earned and sustained by good habits, strong ethical behavior, a positive attitude, and a show of resiliency.

The National Association of Realtors paid a third party to conduct a study concerning why people have a negative attitude towards real estate agents. The results of the study, known as the Danger Report, gave the NAR an answer they could act on. The results showed that people saw agents as untrained, unethical, and greedy. The sad part of the results of the study was that the NAR had an opportunity to develop stronger guidelines and require in-depth training in sales and ethics for new agents as well as stiffen the oversight on unscrupulous agents, but they failed to do so.

That was the reason I developed MarketPros' using the HEART to Win philosophy. We need trusted, ethical leaders in the real estate profession. We need high earners with a proven track record that shows other agents how they can grow their incomes into six and seven figures without being greedy.

While most new agents breeze through a little study, pass a simple test and garnish their real estate license, agents who choose to become MarketPros' are setting the stage to become lifelong learners. They begin their careers by forging relationships that will "get in the wheelbarrow" with them when they are needed!

A new real estate agent, left on his or her own, will strike out to try and make the "big" money they've heard of, putting their desire for massive commissions above the wishes of the client. Most times, new agents have so little knowledge about their community, real estate procedures, and the law that they make fools of themselves when they meet with clients.

Customers won't trust an agent who shows they haven't done their homework, nor will they give referrals. An untrained agent won't be able to gain the trust of vendors or their peers, nor will they be able to regain a good reputation once they fall short on a client's need or cheat a fellow agent out of a sale. Greed seals the coffin of an untrained agent. Their careers are usually short-lived, and they leave another scar on the profession.

A MarketPros' Mindset
People follow leaders who they know, like, and trust.

MarketPros', on the other hand, are eager to listen and learn. They take time to observe fellow agents and determine the right way to handle every situation. They ask the right questions, develop good habits, practice ethical behavior, exude a positive personality, and show resiliency when a crisis occurs. In other words, they build their business a client at a time. In the end, their real estate careers become a long, prosperous journey built on solid values that others will learn to trust.

Remember, in the real estate business; you are not to be a salesperson. You are a helper and a guide. Your knowledge and HEART philosophy are perfect tools to build your reputation, and it will happen as naturally as a field of spring wildflowers after a hard rain. By your actions, people will see you can be trusted, and when they believe you, your referrals and sales will grow. Keep this thought in mind as you journey through your career. You are here to serve.

Remember also that trust can't be bought. You can't go into a store and say, "Hey, I'd like to buy a month's worth of trust," or "I need to buy some trust for my new real estate career." You can't arrive at your new office and expect that every client who walks through the door will trust YOU.

Trust is earned. It's like thinking you have found true love because your new date brought you flowers and a box of chocolates. It might take days, weeks, or years to build lasting trust. But MarketPros' are in the profession for the long haul. They understand that once trust is built with a client, there are few limits on its power.

As an example, I am currently in possession of signed checks from one of my clients. He leaves them for me when he goes out of town. In fact, he leaves me a stack of signed checks just in case I find the kind of property I know he would want. Because he trusts me, he signed over a limited power of attorney that grants me the authority to buy, sell, trade, or deal in any real estate capacity I choose.

Now, that's a whole lot of trust that a client gives an agent! I don't know how many agents out there who enjoy that level of trust with their clients.

Our relationship began several years ago with a $135,000 condominium. It was a minor sale in some agent's eyes, but for MarketPros' the small sales price is just as important as a million-dollar sale. After all, I'd learned that significant results often came from small sales. My new client was a doctor who didn't finish his rounds at the hospital until late in the day. The client and I agreed to meet at the condo at 8:00 p.m.

I could have thought to myself, as agents often do, "I'm not working that late." But I didn't consider that possibility because I'm a MarketPros' agent. I thought about my client's schedule and realized in order to serve him, I needed to show him I cared about his timing, not mine. Since that initial showing, I've sold him over 8 million dollars worth of real estate and made over $250,000 in commissions.

Today, I have access to his checking account. I have all his bank account numbers. I help him, and he trusts me. Though his trust produced an excellent revenue stream, that wasn't the motivation behind why I did what I did. I did it because I try to go the extra mile for my clients.

A MarketPros' Mindset
Simply doing the right thing will increase your trust ability with others.

I was concerned about doing the right thing, and the right thing built a certain level of trust between us that still exists today. I have successfully made my client feel that I cared more about his needs and his success than I did about the commissions I received. Focusing on the best interest of your client, not on yourself, is how you'll earn a client's trust.

Of course, not every client you meet is going to hand over their checkbook with signed checks, but you are going to gain the trust of people who will refer you to other people. They're going to refer you to the people who matter most to them, and they're going to remain loyal to you. They will evangelize your message and tell the world about you. But even the best of MarketPros' find themselves in situations out of their control.

A MarketPro's Mindset
Making decisions based on commission tempts agents to do unethical things.

For instance, in 2009, shortly after the housing collapse, I was unjustly accused of being dishonest. The client had purchased several properties with money they'd received from a vast Florida Housing Project loan just before the real estate market crumbled. They were on the hook to repay the loans and saw no way out. They needed a scapegoat to blame for the losses they incurred. They went after the engineering firm, but it declared bankruptcy. Because I had sold them the property and was still in business with money in the bank, they came after me.

They sued me, charging me with fraud. The company made a point to try to get my real estate license revoked. If they won, I'd be on the hook for millions. I found an attorney willing to take on my case at a cost well below her standard rate. For five long years, my attorney and I battled our way through the court system, taking my case to my state's Supreme Court, where my name was vindicated. I knew I had done nothing wrong. My attorney was rewarded with an unprecedented opportunity to take on a Supreme Court case and accomplished a monumental feat in winning this case. She established a precedent; a legal example, which will be followed in all similar cases in the future. In my eyes, she will go down as one of the most caring, professional attorneys I have ever met. Her above and beyond caring made it possible for me to push forward and make the comeback I was able to make. Though she is not a real estate agent, she does have a MarketPros' HEART.

Today, if people ask me, "Have you ever had a lawsuit filed against you?" I tell them the truth. That transparency has shown others that I am resilient, truthful, and passionate about my profession and has been another tool that helps me build trust.

As the old Mark Twain saying goes, *"If you tell the truth, you don't have to remember anything."* I told the truth, and the outcome of doing so was a dismissal of the lawsuit. If I had lied about anything along the way, it would have tarnished the rapport of those I had built a relationship with and eventually stolen the trust they bestowed on me. That trust is the final reward I earned for living the HEART philosophy.

A MarketPro's Mindset
Trust creates acceleration.

Here is another example of what trust looks like for MarketPros'. I do approximately ten deals a year, where I sell a property to clients without them setting eyes on the house. I have drawn up contracts, helped them with financing, and closed the deal, all because they trust me. I have one out of town client, a retired real estate broker that heard of my good reputation through another client, who purchased two properties through me without ever seeing them. He listened to my guidance about the up and coming location and trusted me without ever having met me. Several years later, he sold the properties through me and made a hefty profit.

Contrast that with a military family who moved to an area and used a real estate agency listed on the base housing staff's recommended list. The agency they chose had just hired a new agent who obtained his license two weeks earlier. He was eager and had a great personality though no background in either service or sales.

The short-staffed broker allowed the new agent to take calls from buyers. The military couple gave the new agent a list of their needs, including the school district they wished to be in, the proximity to the base they wanted, and a price range they needed to stick to. Because the husband deployed and the wife and children had no nearby support, they had no opportunity to venture to our city ahead of time to search for housing.

They put their trust in an agent who was eager to sell his first home, an agent who had passed a real estate test, but had no experience and was new to the area himself. When the couple asked questions about the community, the agent told them he'd find out for them, but never called them back.

The agent was kind enough, and assured the couple he'd find the perfect home for them, but the clients felt he never heard them. The agent showed them two houses via Skype, explaining to his clients that there were few available homes in their price range. After a video tour, the couple purchased one of the options.

When the family arrived, they realized their house was located too far from the base in a neighborhood with no children. Although the home they purchased was well decorated, it had been overpriced compared to others in the community and situated in an area known to be riddled with drug traffickers. The house even ended up not being in the school system they'd requested because of a redistricting that happened two years earlier.

Discovering that the agent had lied to them about the availability of other homes in their price range, they were furious. The agent "guided" the clients toward the home they purchased because the seller had offered a bonus to any agent who sold the house.

Because the new agent had not been forthcoming about the fact that he was not only new to real estate and new to the area, nor had researched the housing comps, school districts, or distance to the base, they felt railroaded. After the sale, the couple learned about the agent's undisclosed bonus from a neighbor and were more than disgusted.

Word of mouth quickly spread the couple's fiasco through the soldier's chain of command. The base commander was livid and called on base housing staff to remove the agency's name from the recommendation list. The broker was informed of the recommendation loss, which cut heavily into the broker's business.

The broker fired the agent, who then left the business. It should not have ended that way. The broker was responsible for training and guiding the new agent. He should have provided stronger oversight to be sure the client was given the best possible outcome. He could have molded a MarketPros' agent with good oversight, but instead, the broker lost a large portion of his income, and the agent felt disillusioned enough to quit.

MarketPros' find themselves with challenges like this all of the time. But it is how they handle those issues that make a difference. They ask questions, search out rules and laws, and make sure they are problem solvers, eager learners, and truth-bearers, all characteristics that garnish trust.

If you find yourself unable to gain your client's trust, maybe it's because your HEART philosophy is out of alignment and is manifesting itself in people not trusting you.

A real life example of misalignment is having a crick in your neck. Sure, you can stand straight and be feeling perfectly well, but all of a sudden, one of the vertebrae in your neck pops out of alignment. That one little vertebra is now causing you a lot of pain. How do you get rid of that pain? You visit a chiropractor who adjusts the vertebrae in your neck and shortly after that, your pain is gone.

The HEART to Win philosophy helps you identify the areas in your business that may be causing misalignment in your life, affecting your sales, and causing mistrust with your clients.

Knowing your limits is one of the most significant ways to increase trust with your clients. Not long ago, I was once handed a multi-million dollar opportunity for a former acquaintance of mine. He wanted me to sell a piece of real estate in a city across the state. I was excited about the prospect of selling the property, so I took on the job. Within days, I knew the sale was outside my lane of expertise. I didn't know the area well enough, nor did I have the contacts that were required to assure my client a strong negotiation effort. But there was more to it than that.

My client was asking me to do things that did not align with who I was as a person. He told me other agents had no problem with what he wanted me to do. His request challenged my ethical beliefs. Our relationship became strained both emotionally and financially. I could feel my HEART philosophy was out of whack. I felt the best thing for me to do was to be honest, even though he wasn't. I was out of my lane, and I didn't want to drive in his. I gave up the sale and went home.

The direction I took was honest and warranted. In the end, I had an adjustment, so to speak, to realign my HEART. I learned that it is okay to know your limits and to refuse deals that are not in your lane of expertise or on your moral compass. A lesson learned.

People will respect you as the expert you are. If you can refer them to someone in your professional circle that has the expertise they need, then do so. It then becomes a win-win situation for everyone, and your clients won't forget that you put their interests before your wallet.

A MarketPro's Mindset
When we stay within our limits, we appear limitless.

We have discussed a few different directions trust should flow. You need to be trustworthy. You need a group of trusted advisors in various disciplines. And finally, you need a coach you can trust for yourself.

All of the legendary leaders and achievers have had coaches. In the late 80's into 1990, Michael Jordan was a good basketball player on a good team. However, after several attempts at a championship ring, Jordan and the Chicago Bulls couldn't seem to win the NBA Finals.

They often made it to the end of the finals only to get outmuscled by the Motor City Bad Boys, the Detroit Pistons, a team known for being physical. One night it was Dennis Rodman punching his elbow into Scottie Pippen's nose, the next would be Bill Laimbeer, knocking Michael Jordan to the ground on a layup. But after coming up short once more in 1990, Michael Jordan had had enough.

Jordan began searching for an expert in the training field. He didn't want just another trainer. He wanted a trainer who could help him build muscle without affecting his game. The Chicago coaching staff couldn't provide what Jordan needed, but as they say, when the student is ready, the teacher appears. That is precisely what happened.

After Jordan's disappointment became the headline in the Chicago Tribune, personal trainer and peak performance coach, Tim Grover, went knocking on Jordan's locker room door. Grover was an unproven nobody from nowhere, but Jordan listened as Grover laid out his plan for the superstar. A season later, Michael Jordan led the Chicago Bulls to victory. He went on to win three consecutive NBA Finals with a total of six championships.

Imagine being that elite player — a household name. Then imagine entrusting your soaring career to an unknown trainer suggesting an unproven plan to make you play stronger. That is the test of trust.

Jordan and Grover went on to have a successful relationship built on the trust they put in each other. Tim Grover went on to personally train NBA greats such as Scottie Pippen, Charles Barkley, Hakeem Olajuwon, Kobe Bryant, and Dwayne Wade.

Elite players, as well as MarketPros' place their trust in specialists that can guide them and give advice that will take them to the next level, a line up of experts willing to share their knowledge. You don't have to be an elite athlete or superstar to build a team of experts that will share their knowledge, encourage you when you need it, or help you out when you are in a tight spot.

MarketPros' don't go it alone. Who do you have on your team?

CHAPTER 9

Conclusion

You Cannot Buy HEART

EVANDER HOLYFIELD ONCE said, *"It is not the size of the man, but the size of his heart that matters."*

The real reason that any agent is successful in real estate is because they have HEART. Maybe you're thinking, HEART? That's kind of corny." I challenge that mindset. Having HEART is not a weird ethereal feeling. It's a strength that emerges from within. It defines who you are to the world.

Look again at my acronym for HEART: Habits, Ethics, Attitude, Resilience, and Trust.

You are not born with any of these attributes. None of these traits are available for purchase. All of these qualities are choices. They are moment-by-moment decisions that continually change the course of your life. They are standards that can be developed and cultivated if you commit to a life of purpose. Whether in your real estate career or your personal life, your HEART philosophy will direct your path and your outcome.

If you're continually striving toward a HEART philosophy, you're naturally going to be more successful. You can't help it. You'll be looking at real estate sales from a different viewpoint than the majority of agents. You won't focus on empty greed. You won't arrive at sky-high sales if you begin from a place of selfishness. You won't be coming from a place of doubt or limiting beliefs, desperation or negativity. Your outlook will be selfless as you seek to serve others. Every day you will choose to be your best self by focusing on the good in life. And that, after all, is one great reason you will be successful! Let's take one more look at what we have learned about MarketPros'.

A MarketPro's Mindset
MarketPros' Cultivate Good Habits

MarketPros' ask themselves questions concerning their habits. What are the success behaviors that are unique to me? Is it the way I care for myself? Do I get up in the morning and perform a ritual of gratitude. Have I implemented a personal growth plan? What path am I on that will mold me into a better person? Do I remind myself that whether I am honest or unethical, people will feel that?

Abraham Lincoln once said, "When I do good, I feel good. When I do bad, I feel bad, and that is my religion."

What rituals have you put in place to ensure your success? I practice several habits to success. Why? Because success is simply a few disciplines performed every day.

1. Gratitude

I remind myself to be grateful. I've found that when I practice gratitude, I don't worry about anything else. Fear and worry cannot coexist. With an attitude of gratitude, I'm focused on the overwhelming good I have yet to perform. If something is bothering me, gratitude takes my mind off my worries and focuses on the abundance around me. I appreciate how the legendary Zig Ziglar describes it.

"Gratitude is the healthiest of all human emotions. The more you recognize and express gratitude for the things you have, the more things you will have to express gratitude for."

2. Personal Growth

I'm always striving to become a better person. I'm big into personal growth. For me, it starts with reading. I love how even a simple Dr. Seuss rhyme can show the importance of reading.

"The more that you read, the more things you will know. The more that you learn, the more places you'll go."

I have cultivated a love of reading. When I read, I am learning tips and tools from other successful people, and when I learn something new, I add to my real estate toolbox. It is another key to my success. As Jim Rohn, business philosopher once said, *"Income seldom exceeds personal development."* MarketPros' commit to personal growth as a catalyst to their success. It's that margin of growth that separates the winners from the whiners.

3. Listening

Making somebody else's day is what makes my day. In real estate, listening is a significant component of a successful business. As an agent, there are many actions you can perform for a client, but the act of listening will do more for you than any marketing campaign or gift you give. You would be surprised how few people listen, but MarketPros' understand the value of open ears and closed lips.

If you don't listen, you won't hear the client's real needs. You won't know what they want and how you can help them get it. You'll fail to build a rapport or find a commonality if you are too busy giving your opinion. Listening builds trust. If a client sees you are not listening, they will see you as uncaring, and they will not give you their confidence. And you've got to have their trust to be a successful agent. Listening is a habit that must be tended to as carefully as a garden. If the gardener forgets to pull the weeds every day, he loses his crop. MarketPros' are good gardeners.

4. Ethics

Ethics is the difference between right and wrong, good and bad. Being ethical should be common sense, but in today's world, many agents lack a moral compass. Few have common sense. Ethics is about doing the right thing, no matter what it takes, or who is watching. Even if doing the right thing interferes with your day, or you have to right a wrong by paying money out of your pocket, the right thing is always the right thing.

I had an instance where I sold a condominium to a lovely couple. On the day of closing, the clients called me and said the refrigerator wasn't working. I'd made $5,000 from my commission. Some agents would tell the client "too bad." But MarketPros' see things differently.

Ethically, I did what I hoped someone would do for me. I bought them a new refrigerator with the money I had made on the house sale. Did I have to do that? No, but imagine the response I received when I did so. The clients were thrilled! They told everyone in the condominium community what I had done to make things right.

Several years later, when they sold their property, I was the agent they called. In the interim, I received several referrals from the couple, references that turned into income. MarketPros' do the right thing. Always.

Consider your integrity when dealing with other agents, as well. New agents don't understand that when working with others in the industry, if you treat them fairly, your kindness returns as future referrals. For instance, imagine that you receive an inquiry from a buyer who is working with another agent. Unethical agents often say, "Yes, I can help you. You don't have to remain tied to the other agent."

MarketPros' response would be different. They would say, "You know what? I'll help you today, and I'll give your agent a call. We can tell him that we checked out the property and I'll fill him in on what we've seen today." That's what good agents do for other good agents.

5. Attitude

Attitude presents itself within everything you do. It is in your body language. It shows in the way you greet a prospect. Even after you've built a rapport with a client, your attitude continues to benefit your life, as people share their trust in you. Your positive approach provides an avenue to propel your day in the right direction.

Confidence is the number one attribute of your attitude. Confidence is contagious. If you believe you can help your client, they will think you can too. Be confident in the value you bring and groom your confident attitude every day.

Competence creates *Confidence*. *Confidence* creates *Competence* and *Competence* creates *Authority*, which is the making of a MarketPros' agent.

6. Resilience

Resilience declares to the world that no matter what difficulties land in your path, whether personally or professionally, you are unafraid to try again — being resilient means you don't hold grudges when people do something to hurt your feelings. That's a nonstarter in this industry. Resilience understands failure. It means you're progressing to the next level. Falling forward, so to speak.

Mark Cuban, an American entrepreneur and investor, often remarked, "*I wouldn't be where I am now if I didn't fail. A lot. The good, the bad, it's all part of the success equation.*"

Once again, in all parts of an agent's life, they're either headed toward a crisis, in the middle of a disaster, or leaving a mess behind. MarketPros' realize that being resilient is key to their future success and work to acquire the knowledge that holds them up through difficult times. Being resilient keeps agents from living in a cycle of chaos and uncertainty. MarketPros' understand and apply the words of J.K. Rowling. "*Rock bottom became the solid foundation in which I rebuilt my life.*"

7. Trust

Trust is a MarketPro's biggest reward. The golden egg is given to you by buyers, sellers, agents, and vendors because you have aligned your life with a HEART philosophy. Everything you have learned, all the habits you have developed, each preparation you made, brought you to the place where you have earned the trust of those you work with.

MarketPros' are trusted with transactions and opportunities some might never think possible. They are trusted with money. They are trusted with making decisions for clients. Their judgment is called upon when choosing a client's real estate, and they see their profits soar!

When it comes to trust, be aware and intentional in this area of your life, as trust takes years to build, seconds to break, and forever to repair.

A MarketPro's Mindset
MarketPro's Believe in Teamwork

If you've been in this industry for less than five years, it's essential you start associating with other successful agents on the same journey as you. Spend time with positive people. Being with people who have HEART is going to be vital to your future success.

An important skill I needed to develop early in my career was learning how to build meaningful connections with people I didn't know or had never met. To achieve a high level of success, I needed to make and maintain relationships for those who might one day need my help. I'd always found it easy to meet new people, but when I began my real estate career, I had intentions of using my connections to make a difference. I called it rapport.

Sadly, we are living in an age where the average agent has more of a relationship with their dog and cell phones than with the clients they are purporting to serve.

If you are new to the profession, try searching out top agents with good reputations and sales in your area. Invite several of them to coffee as a way to introduce yourself. You'll quickly find that there are few agents who will give their time. The agents who do, will more than likely be MarketPros'. They spend their lives living the HEART philosophy. Those special agents will become the beginning of a network that will take you to the next level of your career. In the words of motivational speaker, Brian Tracy, *"No one lives long enough to learn everything they need to learn starting from scratch. To be successful, we absolutely, positively have to find people who have already paid the price to learn the things that we need to learn to achieve our goals."*

Another group of up and coming HEART agents are known as the High Rise Group.

High Rise is a community of agents focused on selling with the HEART philosophy. They haven't been in the business for five years yet. They might not have lived in any specific area for three years or have not attained the twelve transactions needed a year for three years to become MarketPros'.

However, the High Rise Group are agents who, when properly trained in the HEART method and armed with proven information and strategies, will achieve the MarketPros' status of excellent. If you are a new agent, align yourself with a High Rise Group and surround yourself with MarketPros' and see how the momentum you are building will propel you to financial success! In the words of George Shinn, former owner of the Charlotte?New Orleans Hornets, *"There is no such thing as a self-made man. You will reach your goals only with the help of others."*

Every person has the potential to become a million-dollar agent. You might not think you know how to do this. You certainly don't know how to do it automatically. In the end, the slow and steady progress will ensure you succeed; a journeyman's approach to growth. If you're serious about learning how to make this automatic, then you might consider going to the High Rise Mentoring Program I created for agents like you.

With a strong team of like-minded agents, you'll learn how to convert leads that create the seven-figures you want to earn. For new and fledgling agents, being part of a High Rise Group will give you the motivation to rise to the top. This group refuses to stay on the ground level with agents who are satisfied with average sales. These agents are not content with going halfway in anything they do. They strive to emulate the best of the best in order to one day become a part of MarketPros'.

For more information on the High Rise Group contact https://marketpros.com.

A MarketPro's Mindset
Live from the Inside Out

It's essential that no matter where you are or who you meet, you need to be the same person on the outside as you are on the inside. Being authentic is one of the most significant ways to draw people to you and to build relationships with others.

Don't put on the mask of Mr. Nice Guy when you're in front of a client. They will see right through it. We all have occasional highs and lows that can affect our work, but MarketPros' mitigate every instance they have control over so as not to detract from their clients' needs. When a crisis threatens your attitude, try centering yourself by remembering all you have to be grateful for. I call that living from the inside out.

Being genuine ensures no matter who you meet, or what outside influences are coming at you, you'll find yourself able to form a relationship because you're operating from a place of service, not of greed. MarketPros' focus on serving others. Applying this mindset changes the question from, "How can you help me?" to "How can I help you?"

A MarketPro's Mindset
Free yourself from judgment.

It was a positive attitude that propelled me to becoming a millionaire producer in real estate. From the very beginning, I knew that this was something that I could do, and it was something I had the desire to do. When you tell yourself you can do it, you will do it. And I did.

Putting a good attitude to work in real estate is something that requires a real MarketPros' mindset shift from what other agents usually believe—a mindset without filters that screen out small sales without thoughts of possible future transactions. For instance, some agents only want to deal with high-end homes, or talk to clients with a net worth of a million dollars. They consider it beneath them to waste their time selling mobile homes or to first-time buyers. I get it. It's easy to tell why they are in the business. But here is a story I want to share with you.

Not long after I'd made my first million dollars, a customer asked me to help him sell his mobile home. With a money mindset, an agent would think, "I'm not going to sell a little mobile home for $75,000. It's not worth my time." As a

MarketPros' agent, I didn't think like that. I felt he'd come to me because he'd been told I was a good agent and I certainly didn't want the person who referred me to be let down. I sold the mobile home with no expectations of other opportunities.

Soon after the sale, I learned my new client was an investor. Not only did he buy mobile homes, but he also bought apartment buildings and large land plots. Before long, I had made more money off that one little mobile home sale than most agents ever make off of a $500,000 home. I closed $150,000 in commissions over the next three years for this client alone. Looking beyond the moment with a genuine heart to serve has undoubtedly contributed to my overall success and will do the same for you.

As a reminder, the mission of MarketPros' is "Transforming the Real Estate Industry by targeting professionals that exemplify good (h)abits, (e)thics, (a)ttitudes, and (r)esiliency, allowing them to gain buyer's (t)rust (HEART.) These professional agents then become referable, highly trusted, and widely known in their community."

Imagine how belonging to an elite group of like-minded professionals will encourage you to succeed. This high-energy team will reciprocate referrals, share knowledge, and help you attain new financial freedom that once felt out of reach.

Remember when entrepreneur Richard Branson created Virgin Airlines? He felt the need to shake up an old industry and give fliers a world-class experience. MarketPros' is doing the same thing to the Real Estate profession. We are shaking up the old way of selling real estate and offering clients a level of customer service they will not find anywhere else. With MarketPros' vetting process, clients can rest assured they are working with a professional agent willing to go the extra mile for their clients.

As a future certified MarketPros' agent, remember to surround yourself with top performers, and other real estate professionals who share your high standards. You'll be privy to a system that will not only bring you referrals, but allow you to find MarketPros' across the country as qualified as you are should your clients move away.

In today's real estate climate, when a new client arrives in the area looking to buy a home or invest, they may have a choice of 3,000 agents. How will they know whom to trust without a referral or by reading hundreds of reviews? With MarketPros' thorough screening process, people around the world will be assured they are choosing a realtor or agent they can trust.

The stage for MarketPros' has been set. It is time to restore the reputation of our beloved profession. With MarketPros', agents without experience or apprenticeships will be weeded out, and those chosen to be vetted must fulfill the requirements or be turned away.

I know the challenge to become MarketPros' is a tall order, but the commitment to the HEART philosophy will transform our profession, our clients, and our success. If you feel you have what it takes to become a MarketPros' agent, take the time to apply to become part of a growing HEART community with agents who are committed to serving their clients.

As Mahatma Gandhi said, *"Be the change you want to see in the world."*

And that change is what leads a MarketPros' agent to a seven-figure income!

Made in the USA
Columbia, SC
30 September 2023

23555291R00062